Everything Far Becomes Near

Copyright © 2019 by Ann Conway.
All rights reserved.
Published by Finch & Fellow
Publishing Home.

"Ann Conway's poems do indeed take us 'far,' but they also take us deep and near—into gritty places and complex people. Every poem, every word feels lived-in and pulses with beauty and perception."

—Leslie Leyland Fields, author of *The Wonder Years: 40 Women Over 40 on Aging, Faith, Beauty and Strength*

"In deceptively simple and wonderfully crafted lines, Ann Conway casts an unblinking eye across generations of a New England family and their neighbors: parents whose "histories were vises tight around the soul," the indomitable and life-affirming Aunt Gabe, a psychologically fragile brother, unorthodox teachers, and wraithlike, judgmental coworkers. Then she turns that unsentimental gaze on her own voyage into familial deafness before blending these narratives into a vision of compassion and attentive presence. These poems are lovely, unpretentious, and powerful."

—Brian Volck, author of *Attending Others: A Doctor's Education in Bodies and Words*

Everything Far Becomes Near

ANN CONWAY

Finch *&* Fellow

For my Aunt Gabe

I

Everything Near Becomes Far

Hegesippe Bracq

My great grandfather Hegesippe
named after a doomed poet or the first of Christian
    chroniclers
became a father who worked in a mill in Winooski,
    Vermont.
On New Year's Day, 1887
he walked or staggered his way somewhere
with two companions.

Train tracks lay ahead as
Hegesippe stumbled between bluish walls of snow,
inhaling the smoke of Winooski,
as he breathed the fibers of the mill.
This was the bread of life,
in a time when across town in a tenement,
Hegisesippe's children, three to a bed, coughed, sniffled,
among them my grandfather, Joseph, heir to nil, who will
    soon become sad all his life.
When the train began to rumble in from far away,
none of those fellas heard except Hegesippe,
who looked, sniffed, rocked on his heels and smiled slightly;
went nowhere as he dared a pinpoint of light becoming
    strong as the sun.

The train bore down, bearing the cargo of one person's
    future as it shrieked
at these stupid Canucks, deficient fools; as it
warned with its bells and whistles,
(the alarms of order, of the new world of machines),
arriving as, by some miracle, Hegisippe's drunken
    companions leapt aside
as he did not.
He stood in stillness beyond the rules,
made as he was for more than a room under the eaves, the
    assembly line.
The report condemned, said that my ancestor
either "fell or slipped through want of caution,"

which made me love him,
and all who bore
such distinction in their names
(his wife was Aurore, meaning dawn),
but were seemingly
bent on obliteration,
loving the risk of poetry and the Divine,
yearning to align with what is always within reach and
    beyond reach
reeling, mythic,
daring to tear asunder an engine's blinding light.

Charlie

Knowing nothing of fatherhood my father bought props:
pool tables, fishing rods,
a workbench rotting in the flooded cellar.
These were for my two brothers
in and out of the state mental hospital.

Daddy lied, but was used to lies;
He could fix nothing.
In their rage marriage
"I'll crush you; I'll break you," he said to Ma,
drawing himself up as if he were a larger man
who had to kill the smaller one within.

My father's feral muteness;
bluster trips to the Lithuanian club where he sat with the
    Swede.
Bent over in a corner at my brother Terry's wake,
as Ma sneered, "Look at him, puttin' on."

Someone once said to me,
"You could not love such a man."
I watched his words vanish like char.
He knew not the world of the child with nothing.

Oh Daddy,
Let us live again in all the lies you told about a better world.
How at your own wake,
your barroom friends,
how they said you spoke of nothing but me.

Balthazar

My mother was no ordinary.
She was birthed out of myth, out of Shakespeare.
I tried hard to push down my mother's hand when she
    clawed off her oxygen mask
as she lay dying of sepsis.

At 75 pounds, she was all epic force,
my Ma, who had asked, "Did you get the lust out?"
of the pompous urologist, who chuckled, telling me this,
and I wanted to kill him,
just as I had wanted to kill the girl
who once leaned over me to tell my Ma
to keep her voice down at the Coolidge Corner Theater.

Ma was deaf,
Ma with her colostomy bag, prolapsed uterus, anal fissure,
    all the wages of modesty.
At the end, her arms were covered with blue black blotches.
My Ma, a bad patient, deaf, proud and difficult.

My mother was a bad mother, didn't notice when I stopped
    combing my hair in the worst years.
Hairdresser Bella cut the mats out and
I remember her horrified face, but by then I was
    expressionless.

My mother, who knew Latin and Greek at 16,
walked three miles one way with my uncle past the mills
    and river to Classical High.
My mother, who lost all her teeth at 19;
her Irish mother called her "donkey" in Gaelic,
but look back again at Ma, my mother, dying,
the whole force of her whipping through me so I woke up
    shaking in bed as the rafters fell and my Ma shrieked her
    glorious farewell,

"You never know I might come back as a wild wolf!"

The World. Silenced.

Thundering mills, the smell of old tenements:
boiled meat, hardship, age
Christ writhed on the metal crucifix of the Extreme
    Unction kit,
bumped into the cruet with a crystalline ring,
echoes that lived at the top of my mother's closet
with its sachet of dirty underwear.
My aunt sung in the hospital cafeteria where she worked,
sang the old songs to her Ford Fairlane parked on the
    parkway,
her newest, blue and white, saucy and adored.
Kids screamed on all the streets, "Red Rover! Red Rover!"

My brother Terry alone in the dirt-packed yard, dug a
    swimming pool he said.
Even the littlest kids thought, "Is he mental?"

Under grape arbors Sicilian crones muttered curses in
    Italian, prayed for dead husbands, gave the evil eye.
The talk of barrooms faded in and out when the door
    opened, as it closed on tides of workingmen talk, harsh
    laughter of the close mouthed, those sharp-witted
    realists
as pungent as sour beer, spent Pall Malls.

These were the wild men and women who cared not too
    much for this hard world,
laughter at the gas station that the Lombardi brothers ran,
the peanut machine and big men gossiping in its tiny office.

But the world of silence was what mattered in the bone.
At Blessed Sacrament Church
Raphael's *La Disputa Del Sacramento* hung over the altar:
The Doctors of the Church presided, Moses in an aureole of
    light,
"We are one body, heaven and earth."

Dante in scarlet peered upward, his questing medieval face shadowed
by the German stained glass of the nave.
The monstrance glowed, a pagan sun, golden.
Everything was opposite: the pleasures and corruption of Providence
and God's grace,
His undeniable caprice.

How strange that all this I still believe in.
One Body.
Divinity. Ghosts. Paradox.
Green summer again emerging upward through the cracked sidewalks of the city.

Glory

McCarthy's was the drugstore where my uncle, Father Joe, was once a soda jerk.
He never ate ice cream again.
Freddy Galvin had shell shock, went after his sister Annie and she hit him with a frying pan.
They said:
All dolled up like Mrs. Astor's horse
Spending like a drunken sailor
We didn't have a nickel for carfare.
Your mother's been dyin' since she was thirty years old!
Crazy Bridget
She got in with bad company.
Banana oil
A confab
The Kilkenny Tap
Down city
Down the beach
The harps the wops
Teachers are all bosses.
Ragman! yelled the old Jewish man in a wagon.
Tomatoes! peppuhs! yelled the ancient Italian peddler.
House proud, they said of the Irish who moved across the Boulevard.
That old battle-axe, they said.
Jippy my Aunt Gabe's parakeet chirped. All the parakeets. Said nothing really.
Is that so? asked Father Joe.

"I don't like to talk about that." —All

Savior

The close smell of the entry at Kate Mohan's tenement with
the back stairs leading to Kate's and to Annie's upstairs
Petunias and the bridal wreath bush in the yard
Redolent beer and cigarettes outside Riordan's Liquors and
 The Kilkenny Tap
The smell of U.S. Rubber down the hill on Valley Street
The smell of the cobbler
The smell of the Superior Bakery
The smell of Mrs. Nolan's candy store
The smell of running water in the brook on the parkway
The smell of gasoline at the Sunoco station
The smell of Coppertone at Scarborough Beach

The smell of 4711 cologne and white shoe polish of my aunt
who in her pink cafeteria uniform took me to work at the
 hospital,
where after her shift, we bent to inhale geraniums in Vito's
 greenhouse
and launched twig boats on the Boulevard's polluted brook,
which sailed through the tunnels of Providence to the salt
 sea.

Secrets

My Aunt Gabe, was never, I see now, weak.
It was not permitted.
"I had my fun kid!"
"So happy go lucky," said Ma of her sister,
who'd dropped out of ninth grade because she could very
    barely read.
    When Gabe took me shopping,
we hid the packages from crazy Ma.
I snuck them in.
"Wasn't that lovely?" Gabe said at the end of those
    shopping days.

Leaving Providence

When we lived on Bergen Street,
I remember much; but
of them I remember almost nothing. What is the word now?
    Trauma?
Everything is trauma now, we hold it in front of us like a
    shield.
I was petrified, but a father's word was law.
My father 50 when I was born, my mother 44.
Their histories were vises tight around the soul.
Only my Aunt Gabe I remember and hear:
    "You're so cunning I could eat you up."
To be loved is to understand you are a part of someone and
    they are a part of you.
I recall my parents only when we move to the suburbs, to
    Sprague Street.
How speechless and frozen I looked out the screen door at
    Gabe,
incomprehensibly, leaving.
Words then began; speech from them. The Others.
I am without succor but must live out what is given.

II

Silences

The Cellar Window

The narrow window, high up
The paint my Aunt Gabe bought me,
how we colored the walls bright yellow
in my escape room, where I hid, was quiet, was still

The room held the silence of peril.
I fought back with yellow and orange.
"Flower Power," said the cheerful stickers on the brown
    metal desk
in the occasionally flooding cellar, where
the striped blanket on the cot grew damp and
scissor bugs crept near, as after supper,
my brother lumbered above to lay his greasy head on the
    couch.

My father worked nights running a dirty movie theater
to spite my Catholic mother.
There were holes punched in the walls and doors.
Outside was fear. Inside I read and read.
Scarlett O'Hara said, "I'll never be hungry again!"
I watched the blades growing in the window,
the tender grass, upright.

Lost

The shambling man at the intersection, from the side he has
   a crafty look. I don't blame him; he must eat or die.

When I give nothing, he glares. Shame! Burn, burn!

I stare right back, but not at him, at his kind;
through him, through time, to the burnt sockets of my
   brother's eyes, burnt up in his funeral pyre, at his
   remarkable, annihilating protest.

No one gave/gives a good goddamn about the crazy like
   Terry, unheard, moaning in dayrooms, who never saw
   daylight.

Chains in the cellar walls, unmarked dead in workhouse
   pastures.

I see you as whitish bone, Terry, a relic to anoint with *olea
   sacra*, made with oil and living balsam or Balm-in-Gilead.

With care I place you in a parcel woven from flax, also
   living, symbol of light and purity.

You were the beast in life, strung out, raped, toothless at 30;
   executed by Army recruiters, drug companies, brutal
   attendants, bad shrinks, snickering jailers.

Let me revive and create you again, relic.

Be more.

Be more than the sobbing elephant in Roger Williams Park,
manacles clanking, round and round.

It was the Seventies, outside the city raged. I look all the
   way back into the sockets;

see you! See you grow into a tender boy again, I into a tender girl.

Terry, I am your sister.

Womanhood

At St. Joe's Mrs. Green, née Scala, taught us Honors
 English.
How the Sisters of Mercy hired her is beyond me.
Thirtyish, a divorcee, she wore dangly earrings and a shag
 haircut.
Pink lipstick on the slash of her mouth
She loved to shock the innocent, which we were then.
Innocent as doves.
Mrs. Green said,
"A woman must be a cook in the kitchen, a hostess in the
 living room and a whore in the bedroom."

This teacher smoked and swore in the drab classroom,
made us read Greek tales of endless war.
Today, kids might laugh at her, but lacking irony
my best friend Marie and I were stunned.
When Mrs. Green insulted the honor of our girls' basketball
 team,
I said, "Some things are sacred."
But later this woman helped us go to good colleges
of which we, children and grandchildren of millworkers,
had barely dreamt.

Brains and sex had broken out everywhere then,
even in our faux prim world where
St. Joe's was the "snob" Catholic girls' school,
though we were nothing compared to Elmhurst on the East
 Side,
where the rich people lived, where
the rich kids demonstrated
in the time when our brothers went to war.
By the lockers the nuns checked our skirts for how far we'd
 rolled them up,
preparing for the sex we did not know how to have.
Monthly, Marie bent over with waves of awful cramps.
"For birth control, you need chemicals," I chided our friend
 Terry.

In the back of the school bus, "I'm gonna pee my pants!"
the jolly bad girls screamed,
laughing about Donnie trying to pull his pants up when
 cops visited a lover's lane.

I did everything I could to keep myself safe and unseen in
 this old country
that I wanted so much to escape.
But once I visited Marie and her widow mother in
 Pawtucket,
Mrs. Mancini, who said, "You know, ya gotta live. Spend a
 buck! Have a cup of coffee!"
of her weekly visits to Newport Creamery.
Later I sat on her bed as I gathered my coat and scarf to
 leave,
but suddenly felt the warm wet of the course of my being.
"I had an accident," I said, horrified.
Oh, I wanted to beat myself into oblivion then for one
 mistake,
my shame spreading
dark crimson on the bedspread's pure white field;
sad eyes of Mrs. Mancini's nephew
watching from his senior picture on the nightstand:
19-year-old war hero,
forever a virgin.

Remembrances of a Student Nurse at Howard State Hospital, 1972

First the head nurse humiliated her young trainees,
forced one to take off her shirt,
then screamed at her for obeying the order,
a cheap bully test.
Then off to the locked D ward,
where patients lined up for cold group showers,
were never allowed outside,
gathered for meds at the dispensary window.

Later they were checked for obedience to
the ingestion of Navane, Haldol, Thorazine, et al.
Horse pills—I took Terry's once.
The student nurse recalls
probing fingers in mouths, how the patients—
shit painters, aggressive masturbators, declared Kings of
   England and Botswana,
young kids destroyed by war—
crowded around the dewy girls
when the nurses visited according to each school quarter.

"They loved us," she remembers.

Do you understand how our lives are all systems, all rules?
Imagine the grinning lawbreakers, so grotesque and
   doomed
straining toward that sweet rotating light
with the pure gratitude of holy fools.

I'm a peasant, do not think life is complicated.
Light is best seen when it is birthed in deep darkness.
All thanks be to God, the gods,
perhaps nothing, or hope.

Rebellion

I lived in the silent Maine. All was still in the dying towns
    away from the moneyed coast
where working people can no longer live.

The task of Maine is to learn silence, to understand sparsity
    and bounty.
People get hurt and get hard in these northern towns.
Where I lived, many were starved, got fat, drank, smoked.

I saw the hunger and thirst behind meanness, learned it
    myself. Learned aging, deafness, how to be valueless, one
    of the crowd.

Learned to be among the poor at the IGA supermarket or
    Walmart, the old men dragging oxygen tanks, obese
    single moms in wheelchairs

I learned to love the sort of people I fled as a girl. I learned
    down to bone.

There my life grew small. I was an outcast, did not suit;
    remarks about my accent, education,
was unprotected.

Learned that when you are without choice, choose
    choicelessness.

Thus I turned to the tidal river for love, seeing the
    anadromous sturgeon hidden in its depths, breaking the
    waves at evensong, its whole body silhouetted.
The eagle, osprey, the night heron who stood still in the
    Cobbossee Stream, intent, oblivious to the town;
the backyard fisher who killed the cats, deer, weasels,
    raccoons, all the hidden creatures who eked out lives
    beneath a crust of snow.

The finches who came back to the trellis each spring, two
 robins who stared at a fallen nest as I buried their
 children.

I learned the crystalline realm of stars,
learned the free and frugal life,
learned how to look up from streets to see great symphonies
 of birds diving and flying silently above me.

Learned out of need to see the hidden treasures of the world

My hearing grew poor;
I shifted emphasis.
I placed my contacts in eyes.
I placed my aids in ears.
With these, I allowed the world to declare itself with
 trumpets and clarity each day,
as I, renewed, again heard, again saw.

I listened to wind, saw bullfrogs in the trailside pool,
observed the movement of crows, their sentinels and rites,
 their parliamentary discourse.

I taught myself how to spot iron in wood, to pick berries,
 pick up kindling, gather birch bark, make fire starters
 from pine cones, Vaseline and lint.
I raked the roof, shoveled the deck, got stuck in the
 driveway, got out,
knew I would survive.
Knew I heard and saw.
Knew I would live.

A Judge Speaks

"Happy sad, happy sad," a judge once said to me.
"Happy sad all day long."
As when an orange suited prisoner
lost last rights to his kids,
the file seven inches thick then.
Do all these girls belong to the sex offenders dating club?
The man's gaunt and blemished face shaking,
crying his eyes out on the aisle.
Stumbling, spit and snot flying,
he became the grotesquerie of a child.
Viki, the bitch clerk, said,
"They all put on an act."
Why do we, the masses, have the urge to beat and to bloody
what remains of the soul's sweet root?
Or worse, never hear, not just
of the beating, but of the man, the boy?

Puritans

In that job the deity was thinness.

In the break room, any optional food was exiled except desiccated granola bars. For lunch, we ate salads over our keyboards. The temps hid soda in brown paper bags. For your birthday you might receive a . . . card at a conference room ceremony.

One of them interrupted a rare lunch date to spring up and cry, "I have to go running!"

Of the despised new boss, they said, "She is so bourgeois."

All day long they met, discussed, planned and reported, yet people remained tragic and starved.

What was the point when there was no hope in the dead dark towns overcome by woods?

Nothing changed, that was the point. The point was to be deaf and encased in deafness.

To know better.

The place was a machine that happened to be sited in a neighborhood full of drugs and ancient tenements.

Then there was the Scarlet A, the tall fat woman next door who smoked and ran a daycare. No one spoke to her except the admins, especially those with bad husbands or none.
They who ate the soft and sweet foods for comfort.

Driving to work, I listened to Johnny Cash, "Stuck in Folsom Prison"
then sat in the back office with air freshener wafting from the bathroom for company.

No one talked to me either.

My favorite day was when somebody broke in overnight, smashed a tiny window and took almost nothing, but my boss shook and could not speak.

Her daily "what would people think?" strewn over the violated floor.

Dogs in Kensington

The silent dogs run in front of me
outside of ubiquitous Queen Victoria, long hushed, long
 seemingly absurd.
The dogs run, look neither to left nor right,
beautiful and intent, upending the concept of dogs.
No one is fat here
near the palace, the Regency.
Not for the first time I think it absurd what men make up.
I see the detritus everywhere:
the teeming refugees of empire,
the dream of statuary, marble arches, absurd ceremonies
commemorating the primordial and determined.
History's stillness in the men in cafes serving an Americano,
 who raise their hands, who mutely declare, "I do not
 speak. I cannot speak."

On the wide path a Muslim family walks past to visit the
 spoiled swans gliding across the pond.
A large family black clad,
mother in a wheelchair, granddaughter on a crutch,
turning to look at me, giggling, breaking the ice.

Down the Hill from the Projects

Squashed features mean-looking short man
staring as I put away my bike in the back hall.
I should have learned from that look.
A day or two later the back-door window was smashed,
the new mountain bike, stolen.
I could have killed him.
I earned that bike.
If only I was a man and I could kill, I thought.
Then another time,
walking up the hill,
I saw some young black kids,
homies, hooded, walking down,
laughing, brothers.
I played out scenarios:
was it for me to cross, self-conscious,
for them to see,
as they grow angry, but grin anyway,
in a shared silence,
staring grimly at what they already know.
I stayed the course, they were 13 or 14,
budding into themselves,
with the awkward beauty
of children that age,
their honeyed skin, brown eyes.
I looked up and smiled at one,
saw his blinding outfaced shock
illuminating everything.

Suon

My brother's girlfriend Suon
lived a few blocks away.
She had a cleft palate, mark of an unclean spirit.

The most secular of people often still think this,
even if unwilling.

No wonder Suon went to the mental health center;
her parents beat her for mistakes.
When she broke a small appliance,
her brother bought her one identical
so, mother and father would not know.

I sometimes think of Brian,
bespectacled, fat, greasy haired,
wearing his loud Hawaiian shirt and pewter dog jewelry.

How the largesse of my brother
is in his protection of Suon,
how he alone knows that her name means "garden."

III

Hearing

Hearing Test

Once I dreaded you,
all I could not hear,
the long pauses indicating failure.
But inside the grey padded booth,
I am amphibious,
my chambered heart thudding
as I listen to a symphony of sonar:
small beeps
far away trumpets and bumps
some imagined, most not.
I listen as hard to what I hear
as I did when a child at Scarborough Beach,
lying with ear to sand
that I knew was full of sea water,
all I loved and dreaded most.
In a world muted between beach and breeze,
I heard a whale call miles beyond the undertow.
I sensed his questing eye,
his barnacled heft
a citizen of the maplessness
where I have always longed to live,
in the country without test
that of Ysma'el, meaning
"God harkens, listens."

Safety

At the airport the TSA lady is angry that I cannot hear.

How often people are angry at what you cannot do,
thinking you will not do;
a moralism I have learned to ignore, perhaps infuriating
 further.

"I'm hard of hearing," I say over and over, trying to figure
 out what she, enraged woman, wants me to do.
She's a bully, this harried bitch—
angry at weakness. That I know well.

I come to understand I must put my jewelry in the dish.
The woman glares still.

I'm in the vast detached realm of my silence now.
She too is silenced, free to be angry, to carry her stone
 always.

On the other side I have breakfast at Starbucks. Young
 black man saw it all, tries to catch my eye.

I should have talked with him, but I'm far away. I live in
 the desert now, chawing my scone full of flowers.

Dread of Deafness

I speak to a friend.
The connection is bad.
She calls back, I hear nothing, crackling, faint echoes.
Earlier I had to ask a tradesman to repeat something over and over.
I felt that ghastly subterranean stream that sometimes boils over in late afternoon,
for I lack American propriety, that applauded faith in human nature.
"What will become of me?" I think. I am old, poor, deaf, etc.
One tries to reach through the veil, clutching, speaking more loudly as if the other will hear better if I am loud.
People turn, annoyed; the shame of loudness which I cannot measure, cannot hide; that stretching and yearning, leaning forward even if one appears stationary.
A Darwinian sense of prey
All that causing one to have a shell, a reserve,
a midday sick
All faith leaves, for now.

We are Not Deaf

Today all is medicalized;
labels abound, we are willing cogs in machines.
Many accept this like sheep, but
evidence is often thin.
People hold their diagnoses before them like banners.
Everyone is special, but once we were taught to be nothing.
I think of my brother Terry, his great silence,
but after that devastation,
I came to believe in living again.

I love more than anything those elderly Jews in Venice,
    California
I read about years ago: socialists, religious, Zionists;
voiceless, poor, unnoticed,
struggling down the boardwalk to the senior center.
Their world was gone.
Bad enough the dead gone,
their world of Yiddishkeit fallen and desecrated;
silent, although today the old beast stirs everywhere.

But they are not deaf, unlike many.
Together, they are fiercely alive; their passions, their
    debates
about the Torah, about stories,
about the lost.

Each of these people is a spark, fading.
Every day they fight together.
"Teach us to number our days," they saith to The Lord.

Variations

A Maine painter has a strange eye disease
where he sees not a thing, but its version.
For a fishing boat, he sees a lobster boat, an ocean liner, a small ferry.
How lovely, I think, how strange.
Deafness is akin, one thinks,
"What is that first, unintelligible noise?"
Always the need to repeat
I lean, strain, tire.

"I will not let blindness intimidate me," said the joyous late Borges,
blind poet, National Librarian,
who understood limitation's freedom and relief.

The hell with it, this sort-of-deaf woman says and plays around,
creating her soundtrack to the human condition,
a background score: Verdi, Ravel, Gregorian chant, Amy Winehouse, Van Morrison, SOAK the Irish girl. I would never have heard you if not for this.

It's lovely, the banal is vanquished,
mundane conversations one does not hear are reimagined
as sparkling wit.
I substitute myth and old tales for what I decipher of the earth's mystery: rattling leaves are the wind of God;
the trill of the wood thrush is the nightingale I've forever hoped to hear.
I weep with love for the world, as when I was a shocked delighted child.
In this way deafness lets me soar.

Philomela

Philomela told her story in tapestry
to her sister Procne.
They were transformed into birds,
but the story remains.
I learned to embroider, because I knew little of gentleness
and thought it might give me that.

In early dreams I thought of living on a farm with a quiet
 man.
But I learned nothing of the homeliness of home.
My deaf mother, who knew Latin and Greek, disparaged all
 crafts;
despised her colleagues in the teachers' room who never
 read,
made ugly granny squares from acetate yarn.

Today I sew quietly in airports.
Women look at me curiously,
children ask for explanations as if I'm a reenactor of ancient
 times.

No one knows what blood and dark goes into each stitch;
my tales of woe and vengeance
disguised in pictures of swallows and crows.
A more complex stitch stands in for jailhouse rapes,
someone scolding my sick brother to stop crying,
forced feedings.

I am older, deaf, invisible,
but unlike him, safe.
I welcome silence, though
who knows how to hear my story?
My bones wax old.
I sew.
I roar all the day long.

IV

Everything Far Becomes Near

Futures

Years ago, I visited psychics.
One lived in Malden, outside of Boston:
Lucille
We chased her furry white puppy
around the split level
as Lucille yelled questions about guys
I'd never heard of:
"How about Joe? Is there a Joe?"
"A Ralph?"

Such men had green, hazel or brown flecked eyes,
but did not exist.
Later psychics told me about my past lives:
the usual Egyptian queen;
horribly, a Mother Superior.
"Jesus H. Christ," I thought.
In such past lives,
no one had an ordinary job, such as
a quality control specialist,
day care worker or sous chef.

My favorite seer was Roy,
who received me in his small office,
in the accounting department of
a children's hospital.
His desk was festooned with small fuzzy animals,
cuteness in the age of AIDS.
From it Roy withdrew a
burgundy velvet pouch with gold tassels,
tarot cards within.
He said I was a morning person,
that I had an affinity for birds.
He said I'd had an aunt who loved me,
who had lived in a house with a picket fence.
"She has a lot of the child in her," Roy said.
Present tense, as he believed in the life of souls.
That was my Aunt Gabe, who gave me my whole life.

Of course, I asked about Adam,
whom I then wanted to marry.
Roy said, "Adam is like a little boy and
his wife is very controlling."
I was a desperate sinner then.
Naively believed that the wife
was nuts,
as Adam told me.
"Put me in a mental hospital,"
Marlene supposedly screamed on midnight calls.
But they, locked together since childhood,
were deeply allied.

"Be careful of what you wish for," warned Roy,
but also said that
in the future,
I should be open.
I should make my feelings known.
Forecasted, too, Paul—
"ruddy-skinned, sandy hair, kind of a jock…
intuitive, almost psychic"—
who later did arrive in a look,
stayed.
Who did life right, but is now
situated in a black box on the hill.

Luckily, Paul leaves to haunt,
as on Christmas Day, when I opened the newspaper
to find, front page:
a high school teacher with Paul's exact full name,
a coach, also,
arrested first for sexual harassment,
then for seduction of a 15-year-old.
"Very funny," I cried aloud
at the Fairfield Inn breakfast buffet,
to curious looks.

Stupid jokester, I miss you.

Roy, accurate psychic,
you only saw me because
you had a crush on a co-worker,
my ex-best friend's husband, grizzled now.
You are long dead, back in the day when
skeletal young men roamed the streets alone,
their sores, too, weeping.

Harbinger,
like every generation we thought
we were exempt from life's course.
Adam was my ambition when I believed in ambition.
Research doctor, worked on the immune system.
"Long dead," Adam said of
sick children he tried to treat.
When Adam said this,
his eyes were flat as a fish's.
He's 75 now, heading out, bored.
Far away I smell his old man smell.

All I treasure is the memory of
Paul's big hand over mine,
its current.
Sometimes at twilight,
I feel that hand in the pocket
of the patched parka
I wear on walks
past rattling oaks.
Above fly thousands of crows,
silent and unobserved,
gliding to night roosts in the park.

I look then for the large old house
on a hilly street near trains
rumbling by.
The house is graceful and tattered,
has steps of rotting boards.
All I can see in the one lit window
is the blaze of a magnificent chandelier.

It is this house that I once thought abandoned,
the house of an old woman who lives alone.

Antiphon

Lipstick, I adore you.
In Maine the weathered look was *de rigeur*,
except for tasteful hair coloring.

None of those women had a sense of humor, but other
    friends joked about scaring potential suitors with 16-
    year-old hair and 58-year-old faces.

Those Yankee gals did not much like me,
maybe because when it comes to painting myself
I still follow the Rhode Island way of mobster molls,

learning eye makeup in high school from the joyous back-
    of-the-bus girls
sent for reform school, graduating to beauty school.
I wore the rouge, powder and lipstick of my older relatives,
who'd grown up "goin' nightclubbing,"

Aunt Harriet, tough politico, secretary of the Democrats,
    knew all pols of long ago,
Ma, with her slovenly sort of class,
most of all my Aunt Gabe,

Ninth grade dropout, cafeteria worker, who pronounced
Boyfriend Rob a "skithery-lookin' thing"; who called the
    bishop, whose poodle she babysat, when a Catholic
    hospital worker was mean because she was on Medicaid.

Through it all she wore red lipstick and matching nails, like
    the rest of them.
30 years later the lipstick endures in her silent reliquary:
O narrow pillar, crimson flame that declares that I am still
    here.
I am, with emphasis.

London

Everywhere I hear the throb of Empire beating.
At first it was refreshing, no monster cops in riot gear
The stout homely Victorian holding her imperial staff
seemed equally amusing, equally absurd.
But when I looked closely at St. James Castle, I found two cops staring at me.
Attention has become more and more dangerous.
Singularity, rebellion spell peril.
Still, while racial superiority birthed the curdled hatred of my Fenian uncles,
Tom and John, who loved their obligation to hate,
gnawing on all that happened amidst the Black and Tans—
in the new century of London, I find such joy.
Far from my crabbed ancestors,
the African girls sing carols,
the rubbish man joins with a deep baritone.
This is life, not a movie,
amidst the moneychangers and cell phone dealers from everywhere.

Hyde Park Early Morning

At dawn
my Indian driver said it was safe at all hours,
but complained about shiftless drunken refugees, the ageless
    refrain of who is in and who is out.
But now the park is dark.
I had forgotten the later sunrise.
I cannot see
the stately forest, Italianate garden, unlit paths.
For an American, entering feels insane, off kilter,
as in a dream of walking naked through the streets.
But I'm late already and proceed,
imagine awakening sleeping monsters, tread carefully.
I see a bicycle light,
as on the Walk shapes emerge, various, hazy, clear.
A middle-aged woman, running
We are of a common time,
alive, startled;
beginning to vanish.
How did relief emerge from that?
The pleasure of uncertainty, the future
and this,
the shock of the new,
a park in the dark.

Pieta

On the bus a man lurches forward and stumbles down the
 aisle toward me.
I had noticed him, this man who stared
from the side facing seats in front.
He was fiftyish and still handsome,
but seemed diminished,
the effect of his powerful body
held back by a blurred look, a confusion about the eyes.
This man, of whom I was a little afraid, crashes
into the seat across from me, where an older woman sits by
 the scratched window.
She has grey permed hair, is stocky and barefaced.
The man—her son? husband? now burrows his head into
 her deep soft chest,
his body gathered so he lies sideways across the seat;
his muscular torso intrudes into the aisle.
I gaze at the great curved mound of him as his jacket rides
 up so
his pale lower back and even the crack of his hairy rear are
 revealed.
I see the woman pulling him in, her arm around his neck,
 his shoulder.
Her chin lifts, and her mouth is determined as she
cradles the man on one side,
and clutches her giant pocketbook on the other.

When I look around, I see that
none of the dozen or so bus riders are laughing or staring;
instead their eyes are downcast in a sort of reverence.
The daily snarling and lunging
do not live here.
Here, where it seems that
distilled injury,
distilled love
are really all you ever see,
every day, all the time,
on the bus and on the street.

Boomers

Yesterday I fell on the sidewalk.
The breath was knocked out of me.
It's the third time since moving here.
The sidewalks are terrible, and I was staring at a dogwood's
perfect semi-stars.
There was no one around to rescue me.
I didn't have the phone I've stopped carrying.
Walking home I thought of my boomer pals.
Him with his patterned days laid out;
her with the new game preserve.
They think not falling is the way.
My tongue searches around a chipped tooth.
I don't think that.

Want

The strange guy with the silver hair
in his silver square car . . .
After my walk,
I see him.
I know him.
He's harmless, goes to
parking lots and stares.
He wants.

Here people going to work,
they want.
They dress to be wanted.
They produce to be wanted.
It's not them.
It's the form.

You go to restaurants and
People look up.
They want,
unlike the seepage
on the ice,
loud birds now,
the smallest wild strawberry.
They only want to live.
I want to be nobody.
I want to be invisible.
But you know
want wants.

Charity

I

That relentless smile—her mask
In every photo she grinned
her sunny, strong-armed nature.
In the oceanfront house with no books,
"Sign up!" she cried,
for this event, an offering of charity
from our suburb.
Everything in the house said,
we are prosperous, loved, together.
We, small-town people, up from nothing,
have worked for this, yet still we give.
Long gone the old dictums:
give out of need not out of wealth,
let not thy left hand know what thy right hand doeth.
Thinking of how little he was worth
made me squeeze my eyes shut.

I heard a child say,
Say something true.

II

Once on a trip south to Boston
I saw an older woman in Harvard Square.
She sat in a courtyard.
I glanced at her patterned veil, smiled.
The woman started, wary.
She seemed to be from far away,
weakened and lost,
sickened by chain stores, traffic, speed
shimmer and money, success and shine.
But looking at her wrinkled face again,
I saw that she was strong.
A very slow smile grew
that I knew I had somehow earned.
It had been a long time since

I had felt tenderness like that.
I wanted to weep because
I knew that I was good.

Hearing, Revisited

I am joyfully at one with artifice and appliance now;
the foghorn call of my hearing aids is long normal.
Even their dying, which I once dreaded, is normal.
The world is at a long remove then, a silent film;
one avoids, is housebound.

But then I place the battery back in;
(a vague worry about the future, elderly, shaking hands . . .
    discard it quickly!)
Replacing the aids, I am proud as a child.
I am facile, proud of my capacity for adjustment, invention,
    cunning.
I am preparation, intervention.
I spread knowledge, unconsciously lipread.

There is too a fierce happiness at
leaning into the world, hoping to comprehend, but also
    seeing,
hearing what others no longer see or hear.
It's a great time to be deaf due to this universal inversion,
    which means attending to the world people ignore,
    which is everything, as when
I stop to hear liquid birdsong,
persisting in this oddness even under the gaze of a bored
    guard across the street.

I am so far beyond fear now,
as when I hear the delicacy of the jazz pianist about my age,
white headed, patches of scalp showing, his hands poised,
    the waiting, silence.
How did I not know that silence was full of sound?
How did I not know what it was to hear music?

Forward

The silence of deafness is
a pathway into life.
My failures.
Daddy, Ma broken.
There's nothing to do but adjust, go another way:
ignore experts, ignore aging advice, listen to all visiting
 ghosts, all glittering stars in the dark.
My Aunt Gabe says,
"Don't be like all these g-d old people talkin' about their
 ailments!"
Listen to the silence of the ineffable;
feel it through deafness, swaying left,
moving to Pittsburgh, leaning forward, hearing jazz,
swaying right.
It's an experiment.
Pry your clenched hands off the wheel.
Listen.

Notes

On the title: my thinking about memory, silence and hearing has been influenced by, among other sources, the 1977 lecture "Blindness," delivered by the great Argentine poet Jorge Luis Borges.

Borges lived with progressive vision loss, culminating in virtually total blindness in later life. "Blindness" examines many topics related to disability. Particularly compelling are those which examine the affirmative impact of blindness on the poet's life, including new and unexpected creative directions.

Borges's condition was genetic, as is the gradually increasing hearing loss with which I have lived for thirty years. He recalls the experiences of his father and grandmother, "blind, laughing, and brave," providing a model of coping, adjusting and finding the good in what is termed "disability." My models were far less positive, but I hear and see them better than I once did. Disability has taught me empathy, and its powerlessness has given me a certain freedom.

Borges concludes his essay:

"I will end with a line of Goethe: 'alles Nahe werde fern,' everything near becomes distant. Goethe was referring to the evening twilight. Everything near becomes distant. It is true. At nightfall, the things closest to us seem to move away from our eyes. So the visible world has moved away from my eyes, perhaps forever.

Goethe could be referring not only to twilight but to life. All things go off, leaving us. Old age is probably the supreme solitude—except that the supreme solitude is death."*

As one ages, people and memories fade. But they may also return in gentler form, one occasioned by maturity and understanding; hence the title of this volume, "Everything Far Becomes Near." A sensory impairment like mine is often rendered as a solely tragic narrative. But the fragility and vulnerability associated with deafness has given me both an enhanced ability to understand the past and to live the present more fully.

*Jorge Luis Borges, "Blindness," *Seven Nights* (New Directions: New York, 1980).

Acknowledgements

Many thanks to Jennifer Wallace, the main reader on this manuscript, for her very helpful insights, kindness and encouragement. I also would like to express gratitude to my dear MFA friends in "Cohort 1" for their comments. And, of course, thanks to Jessica for extending this publishing opportunity and for her warmth and incisiveness.

About the Author

Ann Conway, a sociologist and writer, has published in *The Cortland Review, Maine Arts Magazine, Maine Times, Image Journal, Commonweal* and other venues. For several years, she contributed short essays to "Good Letters," a group blog sponsored by *Image Journal*. She has had her work placed on the notable list of *Best Spiritual Writing* and her essay "The Gift" won a Maine Arts Commission competition. From 2012-2016, Ann administered Hearing Loss Toolkit, a hearing health advocacy site. For more information, please visit annconwaywriter.weebly.com.

www.ingramcontent.com/pod-product-compliance
Lightning Source LLC
Chambersburg PA
CBHW020431010526
44118CB00010B/524